THE OFFICIAL
ANNUAL 2017

Written by Steve Bartram
Designed by Daniel James

A Grange Publication

©2016. Published by Grange Communications Ltd., Edinburgh, under
licence from Manchester United Football Club. Printed in the EU.

Every effort has been made to ensure the accuracy of information within
this publication but the publishers cannot be held responsible for any
errors or omissions. Views expressed are those of the author and do not
necessarily represent those of the publishers or the football club. All rights
reserved.

Photography © www.manutd.com.

ISBN 978-1-911287-10-0

CONTENTS

INTRODUCTION

HELLO AND WELCOME TO THE 2017 MANCHESTER UNITED ANNUAL.

These are highly exciting times at Old Trafford and the Aon Training Complex. Following our success in the 2016 FA Cup final, the club's subsequent incomings – both on the pitch and in the dugout – have sprinkled plenty of stardust on the club.

The appointment of Jose Mourinho was a major coup, providing us with the best boss around. If you aren't aware of the gaffer's incredible track record, just have a look at his back story over the page. Similarly, read our epic section on the Reds squad, including all the big-name summer signings, and see if you can contain your excitement about the years ahead.

The 2017 Annual also looks back at the club's rich history and traditions, celebrating our record-equalling FA Cup success and our vibrant youth system, while also shedding light on life as a Red, complete with exclusive hints and tips from the players themselves.

After you've filled your brain with all things United, it's time to test your knowledge of the Reds with a series of quizzes and posers, while you can also enter an exclusive competition to win a signed 2016/17 home shirt.

Enjoy!

MEET JOSE MOURINHO

AS THE BIGGEST CLUB IN THE WORLD, MANCHESTER UNITED REQUIRES A MANAGER CAPABLE OF DELIVERING SUCCESS IN SPITE OF HUGE PRESSURE, ATTENTION AND TRADITION. IN JOSE MOURINHO, THE REDS HAVE JUST SUCH A FIGURE IN CHARGE.

Described by executive vice chairman Ed Woodward as: "Quite simply the best manager in the game," the Portuguese arrived at Old Trafford in May 2016 with a staggering record of success. Having won 22 honours in just 14 years of management, Mourinho has won league titles in Portugal, England, Italy and Spain, while also winning the Champions League with two different clubs.

As Reds goalkeeper David De Gea put it, shortly after the manager's appointment: "To speak of Jose Mourinho is to talk about a winning coach and that is United's philosophy and mine." The 53-year-old is the son of a former professional goalkeeper, studied sports science and also coached youth football, before getting his breakthrough when Sir Bobby Robson became manager of Sporting Lisbon in 1992.

Initially the Englishman's interpreter, Mourinho soon became indispensable to Robson, going with him to Porto and Barcelona before branching out into management himself. Brief spells with Benfica and Uniao de Leiria in Portugal preceded a move back to Porto, where he quickly began sweeping all silverware before him. Within two full seasons, Jose had taken Porto to the UEFA Cup and Champions League, plus two Portuguese league titles, attracting the attention of Chelsea. He soon moved to the Premier League and immediately ended the Blues' 50 year wait for a title, then retained it!

United's success of 2006/07 preceded Jose's shock departure from Stamford Bridge, and he soon resurfaced at Internazionale, where he won successive Serie A titles, the latter coming alongside the Coppa Italia and Champions League in Italian football's first Treble.

Spain provided Mourinho's next challenge, and his three-year stint at Real Madrid made him the club's third-longest serving manager ever, also containing 2011/12's remarkable La Liga title triumph at a time when Barcelona were playing some of the greatest football in the history of the game.

An emotional return to Chelsea followed in 2013/14, and a year later he led his side to a third Premier League title in total comfort. Though the Blues' poor start to last season's title defence prompted Mourinho to depart Stamford Bridge for a second time, he considered his options before getting back into management and was duly handed the chance to take charge at Old Trafford.

Though United won the FA Cup shortly before his appointment, the timing of Jose Mourinho's arrival means that both he and the Reds joined forces with a point to prove. The Portuguese began his first campaign with silverware in the Community Shield, and there are seemingly plenty of exciting times ahead at Old Trafford.

2016/17 SQUAD LIST

GOALKEEPERS

1. DE GEA
20. S. ROMERO
32. JOHNSTONE

DEFENDERS

3. BAILLY
4. JONES
5. ROJO
12. SMALLING
17. BLIND
23. SHAW
24. FOSU-MENSAH
25. VALENCIA
36. DARMIAN
38. TUANZEBE

MIDFIELDERS

6. POGBA
7. MEMPHIS
8. MATA
14. LINGARD
16. CARRICK
18. YOUNG
21. HERRERA
22. MKHITARYAN
27. FELLAINI
28. SCHNEIDERLIN
31. SCHWEINSTEIGER

FORWARDS

9. IBRAHIMOVIC
10. ROONEY
11. MARTIAL
19. RASHFORD

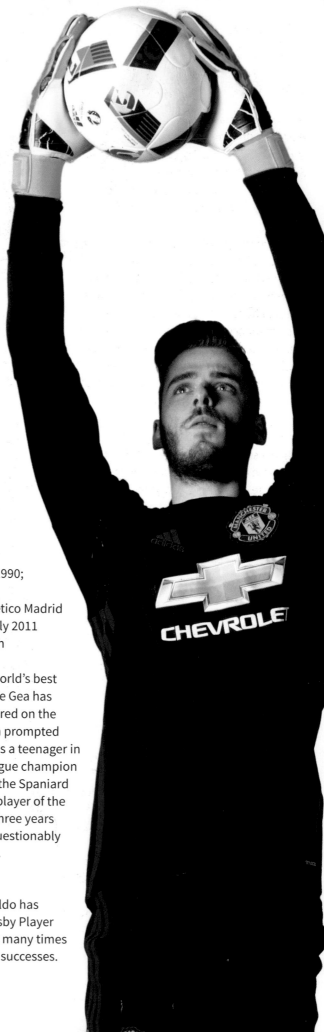

1 DAVID DE GEA

Born: 7 November 1990; Madrid, Spain
Previous clubs: Atletico Madrid
Joined United: 1 July 2011
Nationality: Spanish

Now arguably the world's best goalkeeper, David De Gea has spectacularly delivered on the huge promise which prompted United to sign him as a teenager in 2011. A Premier League champion and FA Cup winner, the Spaniard has been the Reds' player of the season for the last three years straight, and is unquestionably a world-class talent.

TRIVIA:

Only Cristiano Ronaldo has won the Sir Matt Busby Player of the Year award as many times as David, with three successes.

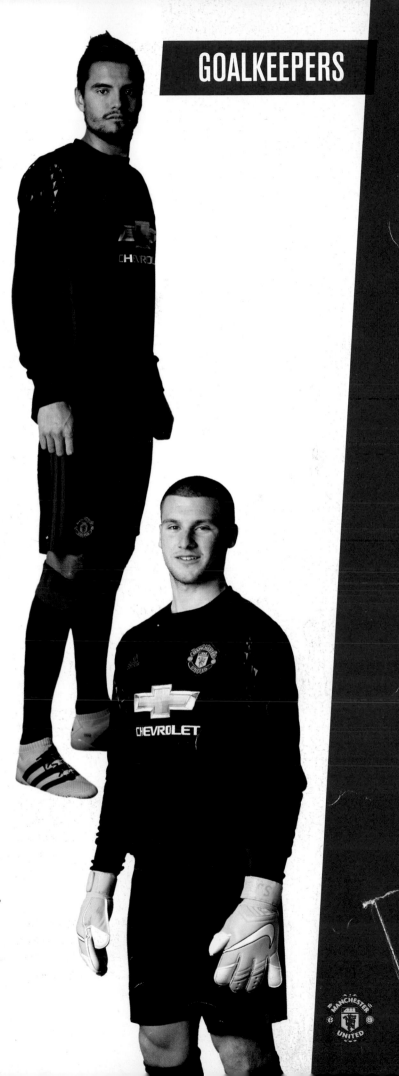

20 SERGIO ROMERO

Born: 22 February 1987;
Bernardo de Irigoyen, Argentina
Previous clubs: Racing Club, AZ Alkmaar,
Sampdoria, Monaco (loan)
Joined United: 27 July 2015
Nationality: Argentinian

Playing backup to David De Gea is not an easy job, given the Spaniard's obvious class and ability to avoid injury, but Sergio Romero brings huge experience to the role. The Argentina international goalkeeper has experience on the biggest stages for his country, having featured in the finals of the World Cup and Copa America, ensuring that United are in safe hands even when De Gea is absent.

TRIVIA:

Sergio is six feet, three inches tall, but his nickname is 'Chiquito' - 'Tiny' in English – because his two brothers are much taller and one of them plays professional basketball.

32 SAM JOHNSTONE

Born: 25 March 1993; Preston, England
Joined United: 1 July 2009
Previous clubs: None
Nationality: English

An England youth international who signed professionally with the club in 2009, Sam is a gifted, physically imposing young goalkeeper who has had time to learn from the likes of Edwin van der Sar and De Gea during his time with the club. He has regularly had senior action during first team tours, but has also shown his ability in high-stakes youth matches, winning the UEFA European Under-17s Championships with England and the FA Youth Cup with United.

TRIVIA:

Between 2011 and 2016, Sam embarked on eight loan spells with six different clubs!

3 ERIC BAILLY

Born: 12 April 1994;
Bingerville, Ivory Coast
Previous clubs: Espanyol, Villarreal
Joined United: 8 June 2016
Nationality: Ivorian

The spectacularly athletic Ivory Coast international defender became Jose Mourinho's first signing for United in June 2016, bolstering the Reds' backline with his tremendous pace and physicality. A centre-back by trade, Bailly can also play at right-back, and Mourinho has publicly stated that Eric has the ability to become "one of the best around."

TRIVIA:

Earlier in his career, the defender was known as Eric Bertrand, but took on his mother's surname during his time at Villarreal.

4 PHIL JONES

Born: 21 February 1992;
Preston, England
Previous clubs: Blackburn Rovers
Joined United: 1 July 2011
Nationality: English

Once tipped by Sir Alex Ferguson as potentially United's greatest ever player, Phil Jones is a versatile footballer who can perform in virtually any defensive or midfield role. The England international has had his Reds career punctuated by injuries, especially in 2015/16, but when fit it is hard to think of many more natural, all-action defensive players in the English game.

TRIVIA:

A boyhood Blackburn fan, Phil was only 17 years old when he made his Rovers debut in 2009.

5 MARCOS ROJO

Born: 20 March 1990; La Plata, Argentina
Previous clubs: Estudiantes, Spartak Moscow, Sporting Lisbon
Joined United: 20 August 2014
Nationality: Argentinian

Another of United's defenders who can operate in more than one position, Marcos is part of the Argentina side which finished runners-up in successive Copa America finals and the 2014 World Cup final over the last three summers. Tough and intelligent on the ball, Marcos, despite having injury issues during his Reds career, is a committed member of the United defence.

TRIVIA:

Among the huge number of tattoos all over his body, Marcos has two which are written in English: 'Pride' and 'Glory' on his thighs.

12 CHRIS SMALLING

Born: 22 November 1989;
Greenwich, England
Previous clubs: Maidstone United, Fulham
Joined United: 7 July 2010
Nationality: English

Just two years after learning his trade in non-league football with Maidstone United, Chris Smalling joined United from Fulham to complete an incredible rise to the top of English football. Now a two-time Premier League champion, England regular and occasional Reds captain, the huge centre-back has evolved into one of the country's best central defenders, blessed with great pace, power and aggression.

TRIVIA:

Like Zlatan Ibrahimovic, Chris is trained in martial arts – he was a junior British champion in judo when he was a kid!

17 DALEY BLIND

Born: 9 March 1990; Amsterdam, Netherlands
Previous club: Ajax
Joined United: 1 September 2014
Nationality: Dutch

A hugely versatile player who has featured for the Reds as a central defender, left-back, left wing-back and central midfielder in his first two seasons at Old Trafford, Daley is a Dutch international with great intellect and reading of the game. His clever positional play, calm use of the ball and occasional knack of scoring an important goal has made him an important player for the Reds.

TRIVIA:

Daley's father Danny played for Ajax and is recognised as a great of Dutch football. He was appointed national team manager in 2015.

23 LUKE SHAW

Born: 12 July 1995;
Kingston-upon-Thames, England
Previous club: Southampton
Joined United: 27 June 2014
Nationality: English

Prior to the serious leg injury which ended his 2015/16 season after just eight games, Luke Shaw had demonstrated the huge potential which had prompted United to pay Southampton so much money for him. Lightning fast, ambitious and hugely capable in possession, Luke is the perfect modern full-back and his return to full fitness provided a huge boost for the Reds.

TRIVIA:

Luke was a boyhood Chelsea fan who was rejected by the Blues as a youngster, but turned the tables when he turned them down to join United in 2014.

DEFENDERS

24 TIM FOSU-MENSAH

Born: 2 January 1998; Amsterdam, Netherlands
Previous club: Ajax
Joined United: 2 September 2014
Nationality: Dutch

Another young player who took his chance to shine in the spotlight for the first team last season, Tim is a powerful prospect who looks like he has been a senior fixture for years. He never shies away from a battle and conducts himself with an inspirational enthusiasm, but is also technically gifted and brings the whole package to any defensive or midfield role. A top young talent.

TRIVIA:

Tim has boundless energy, so much so that he has been known to try to combat insomnia by going running in the middle of the night!

25 ANTONIO VALENCIA

Born: 4 August 1985; Lago Agrio, Ecuador
Previous clubs: El Nacional, Villarreal, Wigan
Joined United: 30 June 2009
Nationality: Ecuadorian

Now one of the longest-serving players in the United squad, Antonio has been with the Reds for over seven years and has proven himself to be one of the finest athletes the club has had. Staggering pace and power are his specialities, whether he's on the right wing or at right-back, and he also continues to provide a string of impressive assists from whichever position he occupies.

TRIVIA:

Antonio's powerful physique owes much to the time he spent in the army in his native Ecuador.

36 MATTEO DARMIAN

Born: 2 December 1989; Legnano, Italy
Joined United: 11 July 2015
Previous clubs: AC Milan, Padova (loan), Palermo, Torino
Nationality: Italian

It didn't take Matteo Darmian long to make a positive impact on United. The Italian international right-back was named player of the month in his first few weeks at the club as his astute positional play, reading of the game and calmness in possession steadied the Reds' defence. Though his first term in England was ultimately disrupted by injuries, his form when fit demonstrated his intelligence and importance to the collective cause.

TRIVIA:

Matteo was only 16 years old when Carlo Ancelotti gave him his debut for AC Milan in a 2006 Coppa Italia clash with Brescia.

38 AXEL TUANZEBE

Born: 14 November 1997; Bunia, Democratic Republic of Congo
Joined United: 1 July 2013
Previous clubs: None
Nationality: Congolese/British

A born leader who has already spoken of his desire to captain United in the future, Axel Tuanzebe is an exceptional youngster who quickly impressed Jose Mourinho after the Portuguese's arrival. The boss said it took just 10 minutes to see the defender's potential, and he looks set for a bright future with the Reds thanks to his striking maturity, athleticism and football intellect. One to watch.

TRIVIA:

Axel has dual citizenship as he grew up in Rochdale, making him potentially eligible to play for England, Scotland, Wales or Northern Ireland.

6 PAUL POGBA

Born: 15 March 1993; Lagny-sur-Marne, France
Previous clubs: Le Havre, Manchester United, Juventus
Joined United: 8 August 2016
Nationality: French

Not so much a transfer as a homecoming, the return of French international midfielder Paul Pogba sent shockwaves through football in the summer of 2016. His arrival from Juventus required United to break the world transfer record for the first time ever, but the best don't come cheap and the 23-year-old can boast an unparalleled combination of pace, power, skill, technique and determination. One of football's most thrilling young talents.

TRIVIA:

Despite being only 23, Paul arrived at United with four league titles to his name, plus appearances in the World Cup, European Championship final and Champions League final.

7 MEMPHIS

Born: 13 February 1994;
Moordrecht, Netherlands
Previous club: PSV Eindhoven
Joined United: 12 June 2015
Nationality: Dutch

Signed from PSV Eindhoven at the start of the 2015/16 campaign, the tricky Dutch winger arrived at Old Trafford tipped for big things. Although his debut season in English football was a rollercoaster ride, Memphis demonstrated his obvious talent on a number of occasions. When on form, his tricks, flicks and skills make him a nightmare for any defender to face.

TRIVIA:

Memphis's talents extend beyond the football pitch – in 2015 he released three rap videos on YouTube.

8 JUAN MATA

Born: 28 April 1988; Burgos, Spain
Previous clubs: Valencia, Chelsea
Joined United: 25 January 2014
Nationality: Spanish

One of the classiest, smoothest playmakers around. Mata has won virtually every available honour in club football in England, Spain and Europe, and he has also sampled life as a world and European champion with the Spanish national team. A gifted attacker who can work magic with his wand of a left foot, the vastly experienced Juan is also recognised as one of the nicest guys in football.

TRIVIA:

When Mata agreed to join United, he arrived at the Aon Training Complex in a helicopter!

14 JESSE LINGARD

Born: 15 December 1992; Warrington, England
Previous clubs: None
Joined United: 1 July 2009
Nationality: English

Jesse's patient rise to prominence is a huge success story for the United youth system. It took a long time in the Reds' youth teams and reserves, plus a spate of loan deals, but the chirpy Warrington lad enjoyed a long-awaited breakthrough season in 2015/16 and ended it as United's FA Cup final hero! Quick-witted and gifted, Lingard is very much a modern attacker.

TRIVIA:

Jesse was just seven years old when he first starting playing for United, meaning he has been on the club's books longer than any other current squad member.

16 MICHAEL CARRICK

Born: 29 July 1981; Wallsend
Previous clubs: West Ham, Swindon (loan), Birmingham (loan), Tottenham Hotspur
Joined United: 31 July 2006
Nationality: English

The wise old head of United's squad, Michael joined the Reds in 2006 from Tottenham and immediately had a positive impact, playing an important part in the club's first league title in four years. He has since won every major domestic honour, completing the set with last season's FA Cup, as well as being a world and European champion. A calm, collected midfield conductor with pedigree to equal anybody.

TRIVIA:

Away from football, Michael is a huge fan of Formula One motor racing and regularly attends F1 races.

18 ASHLEY YOUNG

Born: 9 July 1985; Stevenage, England
Previous clubs: Watford, Aston Villa
Joined United: 1 July 2011
Nationality: English

When he arrived at Old Trafford ahead of the 2011/12 season, Ashley Young was recognised as a versatile winger, capable of playing on either flank. Five years on, his adaptability is even more resounding, thanks to stints as a full-back and wing-back under the management of Louis van Gaal. Wherever he plays, however, Young consistently guarantees intelligent positional play and a deadly range of crosses.

TRIVIA:

After the 2014 departure of Patrice Evra, Ashley took on one of the most important roles at the club: dressing room DJ!

21 ANDER HERRERA

Born: 14 August 1989
Previous clubs: Real Zaragoza, Athletic Club
Joined United: 26 June 2014
Nationality: Spanish

An all-action presence in the United squad, Ander has injected energy into the Reds' approach ever since his 2014 arrival at Old Trafford. His ability to read the game, his infectious enthusiasm and his risk-taking have all made him a favourite among United fans who have seen more than their fair share of top quality midfielders down the years.

TRIVIA:

Ander began his professional career as a midfielder at Real Zaragoza – the club for whom his father, Pedro Maria, made over 150 appearances.

MIDFIELDERS

22 HENRIKH MKHITARYAN

Born: 21 January 1989;
Yerevan, Armenia
Previous clubs: Pyunik, Metalurh
Donetsk, Shakhtar Donetsk,
Borussia Dortmund
Joined United: 6 July 2016
Nationality: Armenian

A truly exciting signing, the Armenian
international is one of the classiest
attackers around. His intelligence,
speed and skill make him a
devastating player to face, and he
has been one of Europe's deadliest
link-men over recent seasons.
Henrikh signed from Borussia
Dortmund ahead of the 2016/17
campaign, and his move may prove
to be one of the best bits of business
United have done in ages.

TRIVIA:

Henrikh speaks an incredible six
languages! He is fluent in Armenian,
Russian, English, German, French
and Portuguese.

27 MAROUANE FELLAINI

Born: 22 November 1987;
Etterbeek, Belgium
Previous clubs: Standard Liege, Everton
Joined United: 2 September 2013
Nationality: Belgian

With his lofty height and enormous
afro, Marouane is one of the most
distinctive figures in world football.
He regularly troubled United as an
opponent during his five years at
Everton, and since his 2013 arrival
at Old Trafford has proven himself
to be a versatile and valuable
attacking weapon. A tough, battling
presence in a variety of midfield
roles, the Belgian international is
unstoppable on his day.

TRIVIA:

Fellaini used to run long distances
to school as a child, and could
have been a marathon runner if his
football career hadn't taken off!

28 MORGAN SCHNEIDERLIN

Born: 8 November 1989; Zellwiller, France
Previous clubs: RC Strasbourg, Southampton
Joined United: 13 July 2015
Nationality: French

Having helped Southampton climb from League One to the Premier League, Morgan Schneiderlin knows all about what is required in a battle. The French international brings a wealth of qualities to United's midfield, primarily his razor-sharp reading of the game and his unerring ability to nick possession for his team at vital times. A top quality player aiming to build on his solid first season with an even better campaign in 2016/17.

TRIVIA:

When listing his football heroes, Morgan names one of his biggest influences as Reds legend Eric Cantona, who represented the club between 1992 and 1997.

31 BASTIAN SCHWEINSTEIGER

Born: 1 August 1984; Kolbermoor, Germany
Joined United: 13 July 2015
Previous club: Bayern Munich
Nationality: German

A player with a wealth of experience. Bastian rose through the youth ranks at Bayern Munich and was initially a right-sided midfielder before Bayern boss Louis van Gaal converted him into a more central role. The move had incredible results and Basti became a key part of Bayern's all-conquering team, winning 22 major honours in 12 years. Oh, and he also won the World Cup with Germany in 2014. He's been there, done it, won it.

TRIVIA:

Bastian's wife, Ana Ivanovic, is a Serbian professional tennis player who won the French Open in 2008.

9 ZLATAN IBRAHIMOVIC

Born: 3 October 1981; Malmo, Sweden
Previous clubs: Malmo, Ajax, Juventus, Internazionale, Barcelona, AC Milan, Paris St Germain
Joined United: 1 July 2016
Nationality: Swedish

One of world football's most recognisable stars, Zlatan Ibrahimovic is a stone cold winner. He has won 13 league titles in the last 15 seasons (though two won with Juventus were later stripped), and has continued to improve with age. He is now one of the most powerful, unstoppable strikers around and his eye for the spectacular makes him a joy to watch. He was born for Old Trafford.

TRIVIA:

Zlatan has a black belt in taekwondo, a martial art which originates from Korea. Don't mess with him!

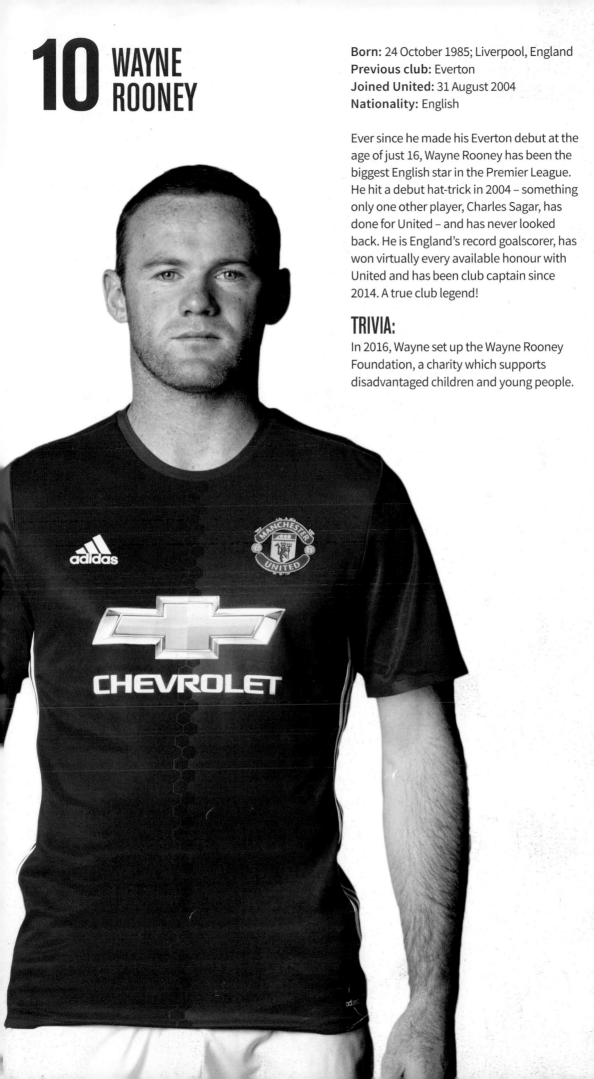

10 WAYNE ROONEY

Born: 24 October 1985; Liverpool, England
Previous club: Everton
Joined United: 31 August 2004
Nationality: English

Ever since he made his Everton debut at the age of just 16, Wayne Rooney has been the biggest English star in the Premier League. He hit a debut hat-trick in 2004 – something only one other player, Charles Sagar, has done for United – and has never looked back. He is England's record goalscorer, has won virtually every available honour with United and has been club captain since 2014. A true club legend!

TRIVIA:

In 2016, Wayne set up the Wayne Rooney Foundation, a charity which supports disadvantaged children and young people.

11 ANTHONY MARTIAL

Born: 5 December 1995; Massy, France
Previous clubs: Lyon, Monaco
Joined United: 1 September 2015
Nationality: French

From nowhere to superstardom, Anthony Martial enjoyed a stunning first season in English football after his shock arrival from Monaco late in the summer 2015 transfer window. His brilliant debut goal against Liverpool demonstrated why United had paid so much to sign him, and he went on to turn in a string of impressive displays as he finished the season as the Reds' top scorer. Devastatingly quick and incredibly calm in front of goal, Anthony is one of the most exciting strikers around.

TRIVIA:

Alongside Leicester's Jamie Vardy, Anthony was the Premier League's fastest player in 2015/16, reaching speeds of 22 miles per hour!

19 MARCUS RASHFORD

Born: 31 October 1997;
Manchester, England
Previous clubs: None
Joined United: 1 July 2014
Nationality: English

The undoubted sensation of the 2015/16 season, Marcus Rashford came from nowhere to become a household name and one of English football's brightest young talents in the space of just a few weeks. Devastatingly quick, thrillingly skilful and charmingly carefree, the local lad from Wythenshawe has been living a dream from the moment he came into the senior setup, and his future looks blindingly bright.

TRIVIA:

Just 96 days separated Rashford's debuts for United and England, against FC Midtjylland and Australia respectively, and he scored in both games!

WORKING HARD

OUR SNAPPERS TOOK SOME SHOTS OF THE LADS GETTING READY FOR ACTION

MAKE YOUR
UNITED DEBUT

"I was overwhelmed, very overwhelmed. When I was sat on the bench, I was more nervous than when I had to play football itself for the first time! Thankfully, the players around me helped me very much to play well and do what I had to do. After the game, everyone told me I'd done well and it was very pleasing for me. When the chance comes, you have to play well and make the most of it."

TIM FOSU-MENSAH

WHAT IT'S LIKE TO...
REDS STARS SHARE THEIR EXPERIENCES

SCORE AT THE
STRETFORD END

It's always special to score a goal, but it was a massive moment for me to score my first senior goal against West Brom. It was great to see it go in, then to be able to celebrate in front of the Stretford End, with my family there, it was a special day. I was getting messages left, right and centre from my friends and family."

JESSE LINGARD

GO ON
PRE-SEASON TOUR

"The reception you get when you go on tour – especially in Asia - is something quite unreal. I think it's the die-hard fans that we don't get to see every week. We get to speak to them on social media, but being able to go over and see them outside our hotel or at training sessions, wherever we are, there are always fans there. It's great to see, and it gives us a great feeling."

CHRIS SMALLING

PLAY 500
GAMES FOR UNITED

"Of course, it was a significant moment in my career when I passed that marker against Norwich City. It was a disappointing day in terms of the result, but to make 500 appearances for Manchester United is a great honour. Only 10 players have achieved that now and I am obviously proud to have done that."

WAYNE ROONEY

MAKE A WORLD CLASS SAVE

"The one-handed save I made against FC Midtjylland in the Europa League was one of the best I've made in my life, so it was a very nice occasion for me. Saves like that are the moments that tell me personally that I'm totally prepared for whenever my manager needs to call on me. It was important to me to demonstrate to myself that I'm always ready."

SERGIO ROMERO

WHAT IT'S LIKE TO...

REDS STARS SHARE THEIR EXPERIENCES

BE AMONG UNITED'S AWAY SUPPORTERS

"Our away fans are amazing and I've always wanted to be a part of that. To go away from home to Anfield is what I did as a kid. I fell in love with the game doing things like that, and I want to do it again. It was just a great day and I loved it, obviously winning the game was brilliant but everything around it was what I'd expected."

MICHAEL CARRICK

CAPTAIN
THE TEAM

"I thrive on it and I like it. Even when you've not got the captain's armband, there are that many eyes on you, at Manchester United you have to perform, but when you have that responsibility as well, it's also the players thaat look to you in tough moments. It makes you back yourself and make sure you put in a great performance because you've got the added responsibility of the armband."

CHRIS SMALLING

LIFT A
TROPHY

"The FA Cup final is an unforgettable experience: the organisation, the pre-match show, the tension during the game. Luckily for me, I have been involved in two and both of them ended up with me lifting the trophy. I feel privileged for that. It was my first trophy with United and being able to win the Cup for the fans, after such unconditional support throughout the entire season, made me feel absolutely happy and proud. It was a fantastic feeling."

JUAN MATA

DREAM DEBUTS

RELIVE SOME OF THE MOST INCREDIBLE BOWS IN UNITED'S RECENT HISTORY..

CRISTIANO RONALDO

V BOLTON WANDERERS, 2003

The Portuguese superstar may now be recognised as one of football's all-time greats, but when he joined United back in August 2003 he was just an unknown kid with dodgy hair. Within half an hour of making his debut as a second half substitute against Bolton Wanderers, however, Ronaldo had established himself as a fans' favourite and a star of the future. The 18-year-old Portuguese winger terrorised Bolton's defenders, winning a penalty, notching an assist and prompting one newspaper to report: "Those who have spent years waiting for the new George Best can hang up their worry beads."

WAYNE ROONEY

V FENERBAHCE, 2004

Just over a year after Ronaldo had burst to prominence, Wayne Rooney went one better by becoming only the second player ever to score a debut hat-trick for the Reds. For added impact, the firebrand England striker, still only 18, did it in style: crashing home three brilliant goals in less than an hour of a Champions League meeting with Fenerbahce. Not bad for starters, and also the perfect way to set the tone for an epic Reds career in which Rooney has scored goals galore, won virtually every available trophy and risen to the rank of club captain.

KIKO MACHEDA

V ASTON VILLA, 2009

Unheard of one moment, unforgettable the next, Kiko Macheda's United career was only brief, but it will forever remain one of the most important stories in club history. Drawing 2-2 in a must-win game against Aston Villa, the 17-year-old Italian – who had never even been on the first team bench before - marked his debut by curling home a wonderful injury-time winner at the Stretford End to spark some of the wildest celebrations Old Trafford has ever seen. Drama, romance and brilliance all combined in the most United of debuts.

NEW BOYS

MEET THE HOMEGROWN HEROES WHO TOOK THE FIRST TEAM BY STORM IN 2015/16...

MARCUS RASHFORD

APPEARANCES: 18
GOALS: 8

Virtually unheard of in senior football in mid-February, the 18-year-old ended the season as an FA Cup winner and arguably the only player to emerge from England's Euro 2016 campaign with his reputation enhanced. A warm-up injury to Anthony Martial gave the Wythenshawe-born striker his first team bow against FC Midtjylland in the Europa League, and he more than took his opportunity! Two goals against the Danes were quickly followed by another pair against Arsenal and he started 18 of the season's final 19 games, notching eight goals along the way to become a household name. The best part is that he's only just getting started!

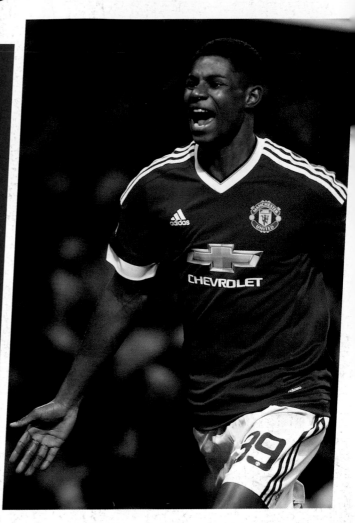

TIM FOSU-MENSAH

APPEARANCES: 10
GOALS: 0

Thrown into February's Premier League home meeting with Arsenal, the powerful young Dutchman instantly captured the imagination of the crowd with the kind of all-action display to be expected of an established first teamer. Tim impressed so much that he made a total of 10 appearances in various defensive positions over the remainder of the season, including the FA Cup semi-final win over Everton! While the Dutch youth international is nominally seen as a defender, he has played so well as a defensive midfielder in United's lower age groups that some coaches have tipped him for a similar role in the senior side.

CAMERON BORTHWICK-JACKSON

APPEARANCES: 14
GOALS: 0

The defensive injury crisis of late 2015 meant Cameron Borthwick-Jackson's career went into fast-forward. He only made his first start for United's Under-21s early in the 2015/16 season, and within three months had been drafted into senior action by Louis van Gaal due to injuries to Luke Shaw, Marcos Rojo, Ashley Young and Phil Jones. Borthwick-Jackson quickly showed himself to be at home on the Premier League and Champions League stages with a series of assured displays, however, and he will aim to continue his impressive evolution into 2016/17 with a season-long loan at Wolverhampton Wanderers.

JESSE LINGARD

APPEARANCES: 40
GOALS: 6

Since his official Reds debut in August 2014 was cut tragically short by a long-term knee injury which went on to ruin his season, Jesse Lingard's breakthrough campaign was unquestionably 2015/16. Fittingly, in a season in which the reliance on young players provided a major positive, Jesse proved to be the hero of the campaign with his stunning FA Cup final winner against Crystal Palace. The Warrington-born playmaker has been patient in waiting for his chance at Old Trafford, having had several loans, but when it finally came he took it emphatically, hitting another five goals which included fine efforts against Chelsea and West Brom.

NEW BOYS

FIRST IMPRESSIONS
FOUR MORE HOMEGROWN YOUNGSTERS MADE THEIR FIRST TEAM BOWS DURING 2015/16…

JAMES WEIR

Prior to his summer move to Hull, the midfielder made a substitute cameo in the thrilling home win over Arsenal.

REGAN POOLE

Marcus Rashford stole the show, but the 5-1 win over FC Midtjylland was also a big night for then-17-year-old Welsh right-back Regan.

JOE RILEY

Midfielder Joe made senior football look simple, playing an impressive part in key cup victories over Shrewsbury Town and FC Midtjylland.

DONALD LOVE

Though United lost at Sunderland, Scottish youngster Love impressed the hosts enough to later earn a transfer to the Stadium of Light.

"THEY DID A GREAT JOB"

"MARCUS IS FEARLESS. HE DOES EXACTLY THE SAME THINGS NOW THAT HE DID IN THE UNDER-18S, IT DOESN'T MATTER WHO IT'S AGAINST. SOMETIMES YOU DON'T KNOW WITH YOUNG LADS HOW THEY'RE GOING TO RESPOND, YOU DON'T REALLY KNOW WHAT YOU'VE GOT IN TERMS OF HOW THEY'LL COPE WITH IT, BUT HE JUST KICKED ON TO ANOTHER LEVEL. HOPEFULLY HE'LL KEEP DOING THAT AND IMPROVING."

MICHAEL CARRICK

"THEY ALL DID A GREAT JOB AND DID WELL WHEN THEY HAD TO STEP IN. IT'S A COMPLIMENT TO THE YOUTH DEPARTMENT THAT THEY WERE READY WHEN THEY HAD TO BE; CAMERON PLAYED SOME GAMES AGAINST SOME GREAT OPPONENTS AND HE DID A GREAT JOB. HE WAS THERE WHEN WE NEEDED HIM, AND I THINK THE EXPERIENCES ARE A GREAT THING AND HE'S LEARNED A LOT ALREADY. I THINK TIM IS ALSO A GREAT TALENT. THOSE GUYS WANT MORE AND MORE."

DALEY BLIND

"WE'RE ALL VERY HAPPY THAT THE ACADEMY IS PRODUCING A LOT OF YOUNG PLAYERS WHO HAVE THE QUALITY TO PLAY IN OUR TEAM. I THINK THERE IS A VERY BRIGHT FUTURE AT THE CLUB."

JUAN MATA

HOW TO BECOME A UNITED STAR

NICKY BUTT, UNITED'S HEAD OF ACADEMY, EXPLAINS WHAT THE REDS LOOK FOR IN A YOUNG TALENT.

1. ACT PROPERLY

"IF THEY ARE REALLY GOOD PLAYERS AT 11 AND THEY HAVEN'T GOT THE RIGHT ATTITUDE OR THE RIGHT PERSONALITY, WE DON'T WANT THEM. WE WOULD RATHER LET THEM GO SOMEWHERE ELSE."

2. TOUGHEN UP

"WE GIVE THE LADS A LOT OF OBSTACLES TO CLIMB MENTALLY. WE GET THEM MENTALLY TOUGH IN THE GYM AND IN TRAINING, PUT THEM THROUGH THE MILL AND DON'T GIVE THEM ANY GET-OUTS."

3. KEEP AN OPEN MIND

"YOU CAN'T BE TOO SINGLE-MINDED ABOUT 'I WON'T DO THIS OR WON'T DO THAT'. YOU DON'T KNOW WHAT IS AROUND THE CORNER."

4. THINK LIKE A RED

"WE ACT QUICKLY AND BRING YOUNG PLAYERS INTO OUR SET-UP EARLY DOORS SO THEY CAN LEARN THE MANCHESTER UNITED WAY BOTH ON AND OFF THE PITCH."

5. SHOW YOUR TALENT

"IF THEY ARE GOOD ENOUGH THEY WILL GET THE CHANCE."

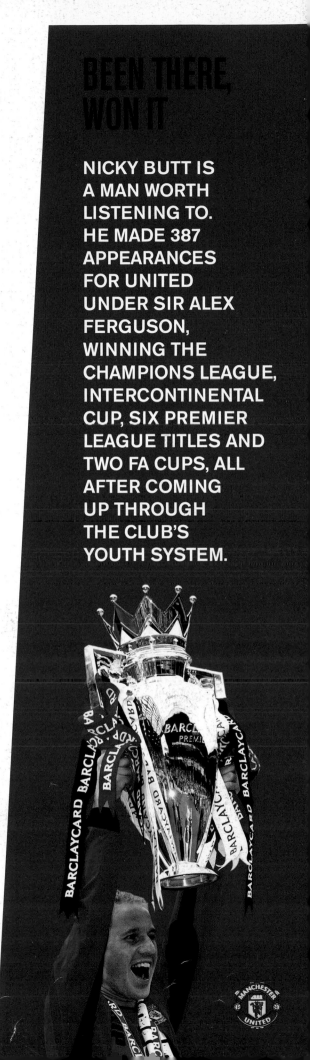

BEEN THERE, WON IT

NICKY BUTT IS A MAN WORTH LISTENING TO. HE MADE 387 APPEARANCES FOR UNITED UNDER SIR ALEX FERGUSON, WINNING THE CHAMPIONS LEAGUE, INTERCONTINENTAL CUP, SIX PREMIER LEAGUE TITLES AND TWO FA CUPS, ALL AFTER COMING UP THROUGH THE CLUB'S YOUTH SYSTEM.

UNITED: FA CUP WINNERS 2016!

UNITED'S 2015/16 FA CUP SUCCESS WAS A JOINT-RECORD 12TH IN THE CLUB'S HISTORY, AND THE PERFECT ENDING TO A ROLLERCOASTER CAMPAIGN. HERE'S HOW THE REDS MADE HISTORY AT WEMBLEY STADIUM...

3RD ROUND | 9 JANUARY 2016 | OLD TRAFFORD

UNITED 1 SHEFFIELD UNITED 0
ROONEY (PEN) 40

Patience was the name of the game as United had to steadily wear down League One side Sheffield United. The Reds were restricted to just two shots on target all game, but the second proved decisive, coming from Wayne Rooney's successful penalty conversion after Memphis had been fouled inside the area.

DERBY COUNTY 1 UNITED 3
THORNE 37 ROONEY 17, BLIND 65, MATA 83

4TH ROUND | 29 JANUARY 2016 | IPRO STADIUM

A hugely enjoyably Friday evening trip to the Midlands, where United's huge travelling support sang long and loud into the night as Rooney set the ball rolling on a key victory with a brilliant curler. Though George Thorne equalised before half-time, Daley Blind's clinical finish restored the visitors' advantage and Juan Mata swept home a late clincher.

5TH ROUND | 22 FEBRUARY 2016 | NEW MEADOW

SHREWSBURY TOWN 0 UNITED 3
SMALLING 5, MATA 40, LINGARD 62

Another League One side made the Reds sweat for victory, but this time progress was assured before half-time as Chris Smalling steered home the opener and Mata curled in a sumptuous free-kick. Jesse Lingard turned in a third just after the hour mark to seal a comprehensive victory and book a tricky quarter-final tie with West Ham...

UNITED 1 WEST HAM UNITED 1
MARTIAL 83 PAYET 68

QUARTER-FINAL | 13 MARCH 2016 | OLD TRAFFORD

The Reds survived an Old Trafford scare to remain in the competition through Anthony Martial's first goal in the FA Cup. After a cagey first half, the second period ignited when Dimitri Payet curled home a fabulous long-range free-kick for the visitors, only for Martial to pop up and convert Ander Herrera's cross and secure a replay at Upton Park.

QUARTER-FINAL REPLAY | 13 APRIL 2016 | UPTON PARK

WEST HAM UNITED 1 UNITED 2
TOMKINS 79 RASHFORD 54, FELLAINI 67

A superb team display and individual heroics from David De Gea booked United a spot in the semi-finals on a thrilling night at Upton Park. Once again, the game burst into life after the break as Marcus Rashford curled in a magnificent opener before Marouane Fellaini nudged the Reds two goals ahead. Though James Tomkins pulled one back, De Gea's fine late saves clinched a huge win.

EVERTON 1 UNITED 2

SMALLING OG 75   FELLAINI 34, MARTIAL 90

SEMI-FINAL | 23 APRIL | WEMBLEY STADIUM

What a way to win a match! United should have put the game to bed in a dominant first-half display, but could notch only Fellaini's goal against his former club. Everton improved in the second half and were only denied an equaliser when De Gea brilliantly saved Romelu Lukaku's penalty. Smalling's own-goal did bring the Merseysiders level with 15 minutes remaining, only for Martial to clinically fire home an injury-time winner to send United's supporters wild with delight. Get in!

THE FA CUP FINAL

It was tense and, at times, tortuous, but United's 12th FA Cup final success was achieved in dramatic fashion as the 10-man Reds came from behind to beat Crystal Palace at Wembley.

Both Marouane Fellaini and Anthony Martial hit the Palace woodwork in the second period as United bossed the game, but an upset was threatened when Eagles substitute Jason Puncheon smashed home a close-range finish with just 12 minutes remaining.

Although Palace boss Alan Pardew took the goal as his cue to enjoy a victory dance, United quickly hit back and levelled when Juan Mata volleyed home Fellaini's neat chested assist.

The game went to extra-time and seemed to be heading for a penalty shootout after Smalling's red card, but the Reds took the spoils when Jesse Lingard smashed home an unstoppable shot in the 110th minute.

For Louis van Gaal, it represented a perfect ending to his two-year stint at the helm, giving him a trophy in all four countries he has managed, while for every player except Mata it provided a first-ever FA Cup success and brought the winning feeling back to Old Trafford.

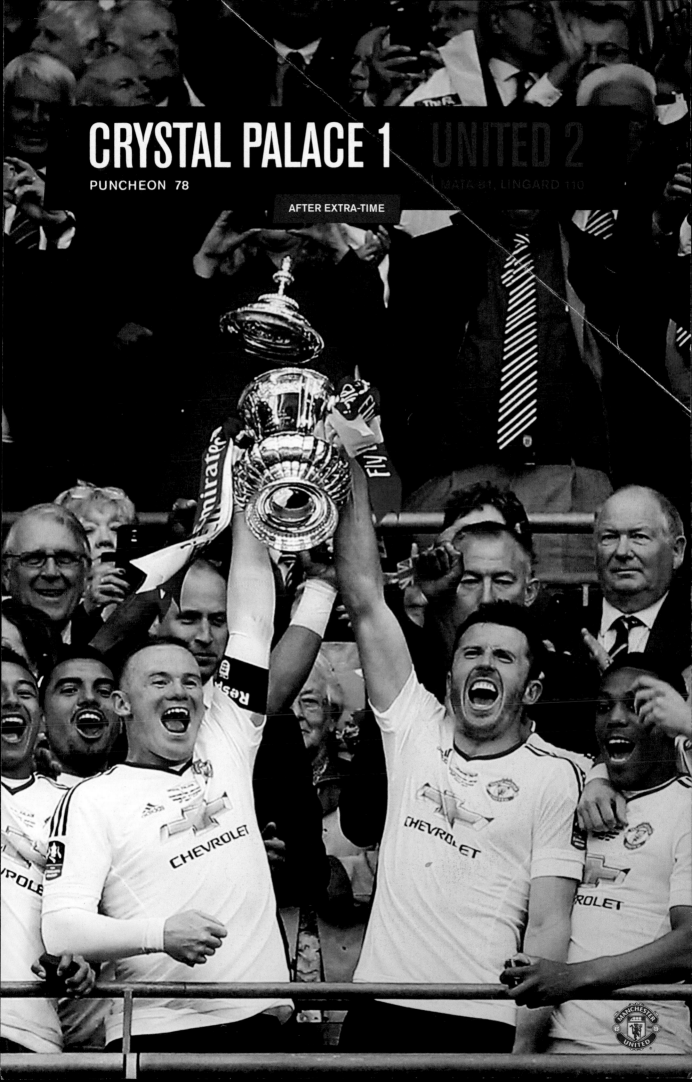

CRYSTAL PALACE 1
PUNCHEON 78

UNITED 2
MATA 81, LINGARD 110

AFTER EXTRA-TIME

SING WHEN YOU'RE WINNING

UNITED'S JUBILANT PLAYERS WERE IN FINE VOICE AFTER CLINCHING SILVERWARE AT WEMBLEY – HERE'S HOW THE SQUAD REACTED TO THEIR SUCCESS...

"IT'S A COMPETITION I'VE WATCHED GROWING UP AS A FAN, I'VE LOST TWO FINALS BEFORE SO I'LL ENJOY THIS. IT HAS BEEN A WHILE BUT IT'S GREAT FOR THE FANS, IT'S FANTASTIC."

WAYNE ROONEY

"WE NEVER GAVE UP."

JUAN MATA

"I SAW THE BALL COME ACROSS, IT LANDED NICELY FOR ME, ALL I HAD TO DO WAS HIT IT SWEET AND LUCKILY I DID THAT. MY FAMILY AND FRIENDS ARE HERE WATCHING SO IT'S FANTASTIC. IT'S THE UNITED WAY – WE HAVE SUCH GOOD TEAM SPIRIT."

JESSE LINGARD

"YOU CAN'T BUY THE FEELING OF LIFTING THE TROPHY. IT'S A LOT OF EMOTION, RELIEF AND SATISFACTION BUT PURE JOY TO FINALLY LIFT IT."

MICHAEL CARRICK

"OUR TEAM SPIRIT IS GREAT - WE FIGHT UNTIL THE END OF THE SEASON FOR VICTORIES AND WE CAN BE VERY PROUD. THE FA CUP IS A BIG CUP ALL OVER THE WORLD."

DALEY BLIND

"I THINK WE CAN BUILD FROM THIS. WHEN YOU WANT TO CREATE A FANTASTIC TEAM EVERYTHING IS EASIER WHEN YOU DO IT FROM A TROPHY."

ANDER HERRERA

"IT'S A LONG TIME SINCE MANCHESTER UNITED HAVE WON THIS TROPHY AND WE'RE HAPPY. WE ARE MANCHESTER UNITED, WE ARE ONE OF THE BEST CLUBS IN THE WORLD AND WE HAVE WON THE FA CUP FOR ALL THE FANS."

DAVID DE GEA

SIMPLY THE BEST

RELIVE THE REDS' 11 OTHER FA CUP TRIUMPHS...

1909 — UNITED 1 BRISTOL CITY 0

The Reds' maiden success in the competition came a year after Ernest Mangnall's side had become league champions for the first time. Sandy Turnbull scored the only goal of a game played at London's Crystal Palace stadium, securing the only of United's dozen triumphs to take place away from Wembley.

1948 — UNITED 4 BLACKPOOL 2

Almost four decades on from a cagey win over Bristol City, the Reds edged a thrilling Cup final to win Matt Busby's first trophy with the club. Jack Rowley twice brought United level, before late goals from Stan Pearson and John Anderson sealed victory in what has become renowned as an all-time classic final.

1963 — LEICESTER CITY 1 UNITED 3

Busby's side were unfancied, still rebuilding just five years after the Munich air disaster, but United shrugged off a poor league season to post a rousing victory over the Foxes. Denis Law and David Herd established a two-goal lead, before Leicester's fightback was ended when Herd hit his second goal late in the game.

1977 — LIVERPOOL 1 UNITED 2

A year after losing the final to Second Division Southampton in an embarrassing setback, United roared back to overcome Treble-chasing Liverpool at Wembley. A close-fought match burst into life in a madcap five-minute spell shortly after half-time, in which Stuart Pearson and Jimmy Greenhoff goals secured a joyous success.

1983 — UNITED 4 BRIGHTON & HOVE ALBION 0 (REPLAY)

Ron Atkinson's Reds built a reputation as FA Cup specialists in the 1980s, but only after surviving a scare against relegated Brighton. A nervy 2-2 draw prompted a replay, but United were far more dominant at the second attempt, strolling to victory through Bryan Robson's brace and further strikes from Norman Whiteside and Arnold Muhren.

1985 — UNITED 1 EVERTON 0

Whiteside was the hero of the hour in a controversial win over Howard Kendall's First Division champions. Kevin Moran became the first player to receive a red card in an FA Cup final, but the Reds clung on to take the game to extra-time, then sensationally won the game when Whiteside curled in a brilliant winner.

1990
UNITED 1 CRYSTAL PALACE 0 REPLAY

An absorbing 3-3 draw led to a Wembley replay four days later, but the second match was a far tougher affair as Steve Coppell's Palace tried to intimidate the Reds. It didn't work, however, as full-back Lee Martin smashed home the only goal of the game to give Alex Ferguson his first trophy as United boss. It wasn't the last.

1994
UNITED 4 CHELSEA 0

The club's first ever Double success was secured in style as Ferguson's Premier League champions scored four times in the second half against Glenn Hoddle's Blues. After a close-fought hour, Eric Cantona quickly netted two penalties, Mark Hughes powered home and Brian McClair tapped in a last-minute fourth.

1996
UNITED 1 LIVERPOOL 0

Another meeting with the Merseysiders, another Double for United. A week after regaining the Premier League title, the Reds capped a thrilling campaign of youthful, vibrant football when Cantona arrowed in a phenomenal late shot to settle the match. A largely drab spectacle, but did it matter? Nope.

1999
UNITED 2 NEWCASTLE UNITED 0

The third successive FA Cup triumph to come within a wider glory - this time in English football's first and only Treble. Newcastle never stood a chance against a dominant United side, who took an early lead through Teddy Sheringham and wrapped up victory when Paul Scholes drilled home. Next up, Barcelona…

2004
UNITED 3 MILLWALL 0

Perhaps the most comfortable of United's dozen FA Cup successes came against second tier Millwall. The Lions had no answer to Cristiano Ronaldo, whose brilliant display contained the game's opening goal. Ruud van Nistelrooy took over after half-time, netting a brace to give the Reds a comprehensive victory.

HAVING A LAUGH

IT'S NOT ALL WORK, WORK, WORK FOR UNITED'S STARS AT THE AON TRAINING COMPLEX

TIPS FROM THE STARS

UNITED'S PLAYERS TELL YOU HOW TO MAKE THE GRADE AT OLD TRAFFORD

"FOR ME, TO ACHIEVE GREATNESS, YOU HAVE TO BE HARD-WORKING, WANT TO IMPROVE ALL THE TIME, NEVER FORGET WHERE YOU COME FROM, STAY HUMBLE IN EVERY MOMENT AND ALWAYS DO YOUR BEST."

JUAN MATA

"HARD WORK AND DEDICATION. YOU HAVE TO KEEP PUSHING."

CAMERON BORTHWICK-JACKSON

50

"IT'S ABOUT DEDICATION EVERY DAY IN EVERYTHING YOU DO. YOU REPRESENT THE CLUB AND IN EVERY FOOTBALL GAME, EVERY TRAINING SESSION, YOU NEED TO BE THE BEST. YOU NEED TO DEDICATE YOUR LIFE TO FOOTBALL."

MORGAN SCHNEIDERLIN

"PLAYERS LIKE RYAN GIGGS DID EXTRA WORK AFTER TRAINING AND WHEN YOU SEE WHAT HE ACHIEVED, IT MAKES YOU WANT TO DO THE SAME. ANYTHING EXTRA THAT CAN MAKE YOU THAT LITTLE BIT BETTER, YOU SHOULD DO IT."

JESSE LINGARD

"MY MOTIVATION IS JUST THE HONOUR OF PLAYING FOR MANCHESTER UNITED. I ENJOY WORKING HARD IN THE GYM AND ON THE TRAINING FIELD, BUT FOR ME SIMPLY REPRESENTING THIS GREAT CLUB IS ALL ENOUGH MOTIVATION TO GIVE MY ALL."

ANTONIO VALENCIA

"YOU HAVE TO TAKE RISKS ALWAYS. WHEN WE GO ONTO THE PITCH WE ALWAYS WANT TO WIN; A DRAW IS NO GOOD FOR US AND OF COURSE WE DON'T WANT TO LOSE. WE HAVE TO ALWAYS RESPECT OUR OPPONENT BECAUSE THEY WANT WHAT WE WANT, BUT WE MUST ALSO RESPECT OUR HISTORY AND GIVE EVERYTHING TO WIN."

ANDER HERRERA

SMALLING'S STEPS TO EXCELLENCE

THE UNITED AND ENGLAND DEFENSIVE ROCK SHARES HIS TRADE SECRETS...

ENJOYMENT

"YOU WANT TO BE ABLE TO ENJOY YOUR GAME. IF YOU'RE NOT ENJOYING IT, YOU'RE NOT GOING TO WANT TO GIVE THAT EXTRA 10 PER CENT."

PRACTICE

"YOU HAVE TO BE ABLE TO KEEP HONING IN AND KEEP IMPROVING ON WEAKNESSES WHILE MAKING ANY STRENGTHS EVEN STRONGER."

BELIEF

"IF SOMEONE HAS A CERTAIN OPINION OF YOU, IF YOU BELIEVE STRONGLY ENOUGH IN YOURSELF THEN YOU CAN BACK IT UP AND PROVE PEOPLE WRONG."

COMMUNICATION

"NOT JUST ON THE PITCH OR TRAINING PITCH, BUT SPEAKING TO COACHES, GETTING ADVICE AND NOT BEING AFRAID TO GET AS MUCH FROM THEM AND OTHER PLAYERS AS YOU CAN."

RED PLANET

DURING THE 2015/16 SEASON, #ILOVEUNITED FAN EVENTS WERE ARRANGED ALL OVER THE WORLD TO WATCH UNITED GAMES - PROVING ONCE AND FOR ALL THAT THE REDS ARE THE WORLD'S MOST POPULAR CLUB...

BANGALORE
LIVERPOOL 0 UNITED 1

WHEN UNITED MADE THE SHORT TRIP TO ANFIELD, SUPPORTERS GATHERED IN INDIA TO WATCH WAYNE ROONEY SETTLE A TIGHT MATCH.

MUMBAI
UNITED 3 ARSENAL 2

A THRILLING HOME WIN OVER ARSENAL WAS WATCHED BY A HUGE CROWD OF UNITED FANS IN MUMBAI.

BAHRAIN
CITY 0 UNITED 1

MARCUS RASHFORD SETTLED
MARCH'S MANCHESTER
DERBY, BUT THE LOCAL
LAD DELIGHTED REDS AT
THE #ILOVEUNITED EVENT
IN BAHRAIN.

RIO DE JANEIRO
SPURS 3 UNITED 0

UNITED'S DEFEAT AT
SPURS DIDN'T MAKE FOR
PRETTY VIEWING, BUT AS
CONSOLATIONS GO, WATCHING
IT ON THE BEACH IN BRAZIL'S
CAPITAL IS PRETTY DECENT!

NEW YORK & SEOUL
NORWICH 0 UNITED 1

NY REDS CAME OUT
IN FORCE AHEAD OF
A GRITTY 1-0 WIN AT
NORWICH, WHILE JI-SUNG
PARK'S PRESENCE
ALSO ENSURED A
BUMPER TURNOUT IN
SOUTH KOREA.

QUIZZES AND PUZZLES

SPOT THE DIFFERENCE

CAN YOU WORK OUT THE EIGHT DIFFERENCES BETWEEN THESE TWO PHOTOGRAPHS?

ANSWERS ON PAGE 60

RED TEASERS

1. Jose Mourinho was manager of which team when he faced United in the 2003/04 Champions League?

2. Who was United's top scorer in the 2015/16 season and how many goals did he score?

3. Which team provided the Reds' opposition on the final day of the 2015/16 Premier League season and the opening day of the 2016/17 season?

4. In what year did Wayne Rooney join the Reds?

5. True or false: Eric Bailly signed for United from Real Madrid

6. Two players have won the Sir Matt Busby Player of the Year award three times – David De Gea and which ex-Red?

7. Who was United's club captain before Wayne Rooney took the role in 2014?

8. What score were last season's two Premier League games between United and eventual champions Leicester City?

9. Who made more appearances during the 2015/16 season: Juan Mata or David De Gea?

10. True or false: United are the only English club to be world champions?

MASH-UPS
IN EACH OF THESE PHOTOS WE'VE INCLUDED THE FEATURES OF THREE DIFFERENT UNITED STARS

PICTURE A

PICTURE B

PICTURE C

CAN YOU WORK OUT WHICH THREE PLAYERS MAKE UP EACH PICTURE?

ANSWERS ON PAGE 60

SHOW US YOUR MEDALS!

CAN YOU MATCH THE COMPETITION TO THE NUMBER OF TIMES UNITED HAVE WON IT?

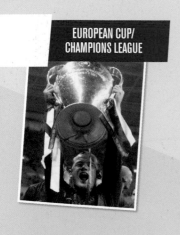

EUROPEAN CUP/ CHAMPIONS LEAGUE

CLUB WORLD CUP/ INTERCONTINENTAL CUP

LEAGUE CUP

FA CUP

PREMIER LEAGUE/ FIRST DIVISION

20   **12**   **4**   **3**   **2**

SPOT THE BALL?

CAN YOU WORK OUT WHICH BALL ZLATAN IBRAHIMOVIC IS HEADING AGAINST LEICESTER CITY AT WEMBLEY?

WORDSEARCH

HIDDEN IN THE WORDSEARCH BELOW ARE THE NAMES OF 10 UNITED PLAYERS – CAN YOU FIND THEM?

```
A K I A A S G Y L
E L C E E H N E I
G A E I A I N N
E I E A R W L O G
D T R A Z R L O A
D R O F H S A R R
B A I L L Y M C D
E M E M R I S M D
J P O G B A J R G
```

Words go horizontally, vertically, diagonally and backwards.

DE GEA	SMALLING	BAILLY	SHAW	CARRICK
LINGARD	POGBA	ROONEY	RASHFORD	MARTIAL

ANSWERS ON PAGE 60

QUIZ ANSWERS

SPOT THE DIFFERENCE, PAGE 56

MASH-UPS, PAGE 57

PIC A: HERRERA'S HAIR, MKHITARYAN'S EYES, BLIND'S MOUTH
PIC B: RASHFORD'S HAIR, MARTIAL'S EYES, VALENCIA'S MOUTH
PIC C: SCHNEIDERLIN'S HAIR, LINGARD'S EYES, MATA'S MOUTH

RED TEASERS, PAGE 57

Q1 FC PORTO
Q2 ANTHONY MARTIAL, 17 GOALS
Q3 AFC BOURNEMOUTH
Q4 2004
Q5 FALSE. HE JOINED FROM VILLARREAL
Q6 CRISTIANO RONALDO (2004, 2007 AND 2008)
Q7 NEMANJA VIDIC
Q8 BOTH GAMES FINISHED 1-1
Q9 MATA (54 TO DE GEA'S 49)
Q10 TRUE, IN 1999 AND 2008

SHOW US YOUR MEDALS, PAGE 58

PREMIER LEAGUE/FIRST DIVISION – 20
FA CUP - 12
LEAGUE CUP – 4
EUROPEAN CUP/CHAMPIONS LEAGUE 3
CLUB WORLD CUP/INTERCONTINENTAL CUP - 2

SPOT THE BALL, PAGE 58

WORDSEARCH, PAGE 59

FANCY WINNING THE NEW UNITED SHIRT FOR THE 2016/17 SEASON, SIGNED BY SOME OF YOUR FAVOURITE PLAYERS?

THEN ANSWER THIS SIMPLE QUESTION.

ZLATAN IBRAHIMOVIC ARRIVED AT OLD TRAFFORD IN 2016 – BUT WITH WHICH SWEDISH CLUB DID THE STRIKER BEGIN HIS PROFESSIONAL CAREER?

ENTER BY VISITING: MANUTD.COM/ANNUAL2017